Farm Crops!
Plants That Grow on Farms

(Farming for Kids)

Children's Books on Farm Life

Left Brain Kids

Educational Books for Children

KIDS, DO YOU HAVE GREEN THUMBS? DO YOU HAVE GARDENS AT HOME AND GROW DIFFERENT PLANTS?

WHAT DO FARMERS GROW? WHAT CROPS CAN WE GET FROM FARMS?

In this lesson we will learn about some crops that grow on farms. Crops are cultivated plants that are harvested mainly for food and other uses, like fuel and material for making clothes.

Humans and animals may benefit from the crops. Harvesting is reaping the fruits of your hard labor.

BEANS

These crops are vines and they need a structure to climb or creep on. Children are fond of using the pole bean structures as their secret hiding places when they play. 256312699

BEETS

Kids love them for their nutritious roots. They are root crops. Harvesting them is like digging buried treasures. They are boiled, pickled and baked. Their leaves are also edible. Their roots should be harvested while young, for when they grow too large they tend to be tough and fibrous.

CARROTS

Carrots are root crops. They are vegetables which are best grown in the spring and late summer. Their growth is like magic for they grow underground.

CUCUMBERS

Cucumbers are planted from seeds. They have to be given enough space to grow. They have to be harvested when they are young and tender. If they turn yellow, they are not tasty any more.

LETTUCE AND THE LEAFY GREENS

The leafy greens are usually fast crops. They are known to quickly germinate. So, harvesting them comes very soon after planting.

Within 28 days, the young leaves can be harvested. Their full maturity is around 40 to 50 days. Cool weather is quite fine for the leafy greens.

They do well in the spring and in the fall. Farmers usually plant the leafy greens in a straight row so they can harvest them easily.

PEPPERS

Some farmers would tend to buy seedlings. Others prefer to start seeds in the house and then move the young plants to the garden. Children love the sweet bell peppers. Adults may prefer the small, hot ones.

RADISH

Radish is a fast crop. It can be harvested in 20 to 30 days. It can be planted from seed. They should be planted in the spring and late summer to enjoy a mild flavor. Radishes taste hotter when they're planted in warmer weather.

TOMATOES

Growing tomatoes by seeds usually start in the house. Some would tend to buy seedlings in garden centers.

SPINACH

Spinach is packed with vitamins A and C, iron and calcium. It grows perfectly in the cool temperatures of spring and fall. It grows easily and quickly. It can be harvested if it has 5 to 6 leaves.

BROCCOLI

People really like broccoli's green and immature flower buds. It is high in nutritional value. This is a tasty treats for kids of all ages. It has to be grown in cool weather to ensure a good harvest.

CABBAGE

It's fun to peel and eat a cabbage's tightly clustered leaves. They are in different colors and sizes. They can be eaten cooked or raw.

ONIONS

Onions are a universal seasoning. We can grow both the edible bulbs and green tops. They come in different colors, shapes and flavors.

PEANUTS

They have bright yellow flowers which touch the ground after pollination. The fruits, or peanuts, develop underground.

SUNFLOWERS

Children love their cheerful flowers. They are grown easily. Their edible seeds and seed oil make this plant even more useful. Unopened buds of sunflowers can also be eaten. The flower petals taste bittersweet.

WATERMELONS

Melons grow best in summertime. They are usually planted in hills. They should be given enough lot of space because each plant spreads very wide.

These crops grow fairly quickly. Children find it fun to plant crops with big seeds that are easy to handle. These edible plants are tasty. Kids and grownups alike love them.

We should carefully choose the right crops to plant, whether they are cool season or warm season plants. By doing this, we can have a good harvest no matter where our garden is.

Made in the USA
Las Vegas, NV
13 June 2021